INSIDE THE
CORN
INDUSTRY

by Andrea Pelleschi

Content Consultant

Ron Heiniger, PhD

Professor of Crop Science and Cropping Systems Specialist
North Carolina State University

Essential Library

An Imprint of Abdo Publishing | abdopublishing.com

abdopublishing.com

Published by Abdo Publishing, a division of ABDO, PO Box 398166, Minneapolis, Minnesota 55439. Copyright © 2017 by Abdo Consulting Group, Inc. International copyrights reserved in all countries. No part of this book may be reproduced in any form without written permission from the publisher. Essential Library™ is a trademark and logo of Abdo Publishing.

Printed in the United States of America, North Mankato, Minnesota
102016
012017

Cover Photo: Jon Bilous/Shutterstock Images
Interior Photos: Tim Robbins Mint Images/Newscom, 4; Travis Heying/Wichita Eagle/TNS/Newscom, 7; Shutterstock Images, 8; Red Line Editorial, 11, 31, 74, 96–97; Diane Johnson/DanitaDelimont.com "Danita Delimont Photography"/Newscom, 12; Ann Ronan Picture Library Heritage Images/Newscom, 14; North Wind Picture Archives, 16, 18, 20; Library of Congress, 22, 34; Everett Collection/Newscom, 24; SimplyCreativePhotography/iStockphoto, 27; Seth Perlman/AP Images, 28–29, 52, 80; AP Images, 37; Gary Emord-Netzley/The Messenger-Inquirer/AP Images, 38; Jim West imageBROKER/Newscom, 40, 93; L. G. Patterson/AP Images, 42; iStockphoto, 45; Bill Barksdale/Newscom, 47; Glen Stubbe/ZUMA Press/Newscom, 48; Kevin G. Hall/MCT/Newscom, 50; Kencana Studio/Shutterstock Images, 55; Oliver Bunic/Bloomberg/Getty Images, 56; Arno Burgi/picture-alliance/dpa/AP Images, 58; Mark Cowan/UPI/Newscom, 60; Diego Azubel/EPA/Newscom, 64; Alex Milan Tracy/Sipa USA/AP Images, 66, 88; Bernard Jaubert imageBROKER/Newscom, 68; Brant Sanderlin/Atlanta Journal-Constitution/TNS/Newscom, 70; USDA, 72; Brian Peterson/ZumaPress/Newscom, 75; J. Alex Cooney/SIPA/Newscom, 78; Jeff Chiu/AP Images, 82; Rod Sanford/The State Journal/AP Images, 84; Imagine China/Newscom, 86; Denis Poroy/AP Images, 95

Editor: Jon Westmark
Series Designer: Craig Hinton

Publisher's Cataloging-in-Publication Data

Names: Pelleschi, Andrea, author.
Title: Inside the corn industry / by Andrea Pelleschi.
Description: Minneapolis, MN : Abdo Publishing, 2017. | Series: Big business |
    Includes bibliographical references and index.
Identifiers: LCCN 2016945198 | ISBN 9781680783698 (lib. bdg.) |
    ISBN 9781680797220 (ebook)
Subjects: LCSH: Corn industry and trade--Juvenile literature. | Corn products--
    Juvenile literature.
Classification: DDC 338--dc23
LC record available at http://lccn.loc.gov/2016945198

Contents

1 | FAMILY FARMS

Phillip Haynie II considers it an honor and a privilege to be an American farmer. His farm, in Reedville, Virginia, was founded in 1867 when his great-great-grandfather, Reverend Robert Haynie, bought 60 acres (24 ha) of land. Since then, each generation of the Haynie family has inherited the farm and added to it. Today, the farm covers thousands of acres and produces corn, soybeans, wheat, and barley.

Haynie takes care of the business management. His wife Gail and their son and daughter are also heavily involved in the operation. Phillip Haynie III is particularly proud to be a part of the heritage of his family's business. "It's an honor to ride across the fields in my air-conditioned cab and reflect on the fact that my great-grandfather pulled a plow with a mule across that same ground," he says.[1]

April Hemmes runs her family's 100-year-old farm in Hampton, Iowa, largely on her own. While her husband works in town, Hemmes grows grain and raises approximately 30 cows on 1,000 acres (405 ha). Hemmes is a project leader as well as her county's soil and water commissioner. She also helps teach women in Uganda about farming.

Many farm owners operate farms that have been in their families for generations.

"I think that farm women are probably some of the most underrecognized people out there," Hemmes says. "A lot of women . . . say, 'I don't farm, I just do the books,' which is really a vital part of farming and every little bit counts whether they market or do the books or drive the tractor or bring lunch to the fields."[2] In 2011, Hemmes's daughter nominated her for Midwest Farm Mom of the Year, which she won.

4-H Clubs

In 1902, 4-H clubs began as simple Corn Growing Clubs or Tomato Clubs in Clark County, Ohio. The purpose of the clubs was to encourage young people to experiment with crops and share their findings with adults. The clubs also served as a way to connect public schools with rural communities and to develop new technology. In 1910, a clover pin was created to signify the four *H*s of head, heart, hands, and health, which represents the clubs' values. In 1912, the name became 4-H clubs. Today, 4-H clubs do much more than experiment with agriculture. Open to children ages eight and up, they provide free programs in gardening, animal science, ecology, rocketry, cooking, and robotics.

WHY FAMILY FARMS?

Unlike some big-business industries, the corn industry begins with family-owned businesses. Family farms produce more than 90 percent of all corn grown in the United States.[3] Located mainly in Iowa, Illinois, Indiana, South Dakota, Nebraska, Ohio, and Kentucky, there are approximately 400,000 US family farms.[4]

Farming involves large investments of time and money, especially during planting and harvesting, when farmers consistently work long hours for seven days a week. Despite the challenges of growing and maintaining crops, effective financial decision-making can make farming economically rewarding for families. Farming allows flexibility in

Children on family farms often learn to farm while growing up.

Farming equipment often requires a large-scale upfront investment.

acquiring expensive equipment and hiring workers. If a family does not want to buy machinery that could cost millions of dollars, it can rent the equipment or hire outside companies to do some of the work, such as preparing fields or harvesting crops. This strategy makes the risk of starting a new farm relatively low. However, if farmers do want to purchase their own equipment, they can benefit from economy of scale. This means that the more land a farmer has, the less expensive it is to farm. For instance, the same combine can harvest 1,000 acres (405 ha) or 2,000 acres (810 ha). The cost to farm each acre goes down the more land the farmer owns.

Family farming works well for other reasons. For example, corn farming requires people to be knowledgeable about the local soil, nutrients, pests, and weather. Family farmers have this knowledge because they live where they work. They are flexible, and they can adapt quickly to changing conditions in production, weather, or crop prices. Plus, farming is seasonal work, and families can take on extra jobs during the off-season more easily than a corporation can shift its workforce.

In addition, because family farms are often passed down from generation to generation, the farmers have a big investment in making their business successful. To family farmers, farming is a way of life.

BEYOND FAMILY FARMS

Growing corn does more than provide a way of life for farmers. It also affects their communities, the country, and the world. Because family farmers are often tied to single locations, they tend to develop deep roots within communities. Sharon Perry, an Illinois corn farmer, enjoys getting involved with other women in her community. She attends conferences with female farmers and also with the Chicago Farmers association. Farmer Shirley Smith appreciates the way farmers look out for each other. Once, when she was renting her farm, the renters offered to pay more rent after they had a good crop. The reason they gave was that it was only fair.

The United States is the world's largest corn grower and exporter. It is responsible for approximately 40 percent of the world corn trade.[5] In 2015, US farmers devoted enough land to growing corn—more than 90 million acres (36 million ha)—to cover all of Germany.[6] These corn crops were worth almost $50 billion, more than any other crop grown in the United States, including soybeans, wheat, sorghum, barley, and oats.[7] Because of the high demand for ethanol, a fuel made from corn, corn prices have risen. Farmers have taken advantage of the increase to devote more land to growing corn. And even though the number of grain farms has fallen, the size of the farms themselves has gone up. In addition, greater technology has increased production and crop yields.

But the corn industry extends far beyond growing and selling. It encompasses many different businesses and products. It involves scientists who develop new seeds. It contains distilleries that make ethanol. It includes manufacturers that make cereal, tortilla chips, graham crackers, and a

Types of Corn

Dent corn, or field corn, is the most common type of corn grown in the United States. Called dent corn because of a characteristic dent in the kernels, this corn can be grown easily and processed into most of the products that form the corn industry, such as ethanol, cattle feed, and corn syrup. Other types of corn grown in the United States include:

► flour corn, a soft-kerneled corn that can easily be ground into flour

► flint corn, a hard-kerneled corn that comes in many colors

► popcorn, a type of flint corn that explosively turns inside out when heated

► green corn, an immature, sweet corn

► baby corn, a type of corn that is picked before the ears can be pollinated

myriad of other corn products. It comprises retailers such as grocery stores, in which three out of four food items contain corn.[8] And it involves the consumers, who often purchase corn products without knowing they contain corn.

US Crops by Area Farmed

As shown in this circle graph, more US land is devoted to harvesting corn than any other crop.

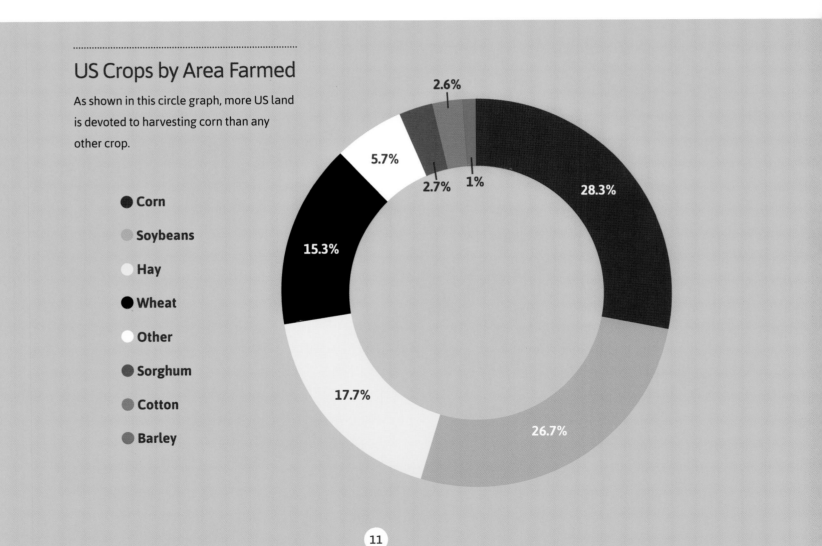

- ● Corn
- ● Soybeans
- ○ Hay
- ● Wheat
- ○ Other
- ● Sorghum
- ● Cotton
- ● Barley

2.6%
5.7%
2.7%   1%
28.3%
15.3%
17.7%
26.7%

2 | FORMING THE CORN BELT

As early as 8000 BCE, corn began growing as a type of wild grass called teosinte in Central America or Mexico. Evidence shows the teosinte was bred into a plant similar to corn between 6,000 and 8,000 years ago. Then, approximately 3,000 years ago, it changed even more and began to closely resemble the corn of today with long ears and woody cobs.

THROUGHOUT THE AMERICAS

There are signs farmers began planting and harvesting corn in the areas of modern-day Guatemala, Peru, and Argentina as early as 4000 BCE. Trade routes carried corn farther into South America, up into North America, and east into the Caribbean Islands. Native peoples throughout the Americas, including the cliff dwellers in the American Southwest, the mound builders in the Mississippi River valley, and the Incas in Peru, grew to rely on corn as a staple in their diets. By 500 CE, corn had traveled as far as what is now upstate New York, where the Iroquois grew it.

BROUGHT TO EUROPE

In 1492, Christopher Columbus learned about corn from the native Taino people who lived in present-day Cuba,

The Incas used terraced fields to grow crops on slopes.

Jamaica, Hispaniola, and the Virgin Islands. Columbus found the taste pleasing and was impressed with how well it grew. Along with gold dust and other treasures from his voyage, Columbus took corn seeds back home with him to Spain. The Taino did not call it corn, however. They called it *mahiz*, which became *maíz* when translated into Spanish. Later, English-speaking people turned the word into *maize*, which became the common word for corn until the 1700s.

In Spain, corn became a popular grain, especially with poor people. It could grow quickly and easily in different environments. It was also less expensive than other grains because it was too new to be taxed by the government. As travel between the Americas, Europe, Africa, and Asia increased, corn spread around the world.

In 1519, explorer Ferdinand Magellan carried corn seeds with him on his trip around the world. As he made stops during his voyage, he gave seeds to the people he met, such as those in China and the Philippines. This enabled corn to become an important crop in those areas. There was one problem with corn, though. Without being processed, it lacked the vitamin niacin. Eating a

Maize God

The Maya worshiped many gods. Some were human in form, some were animals, and one god was based on corn. Called the maize god, he was thought to be a handsome young man with a head that resembled an ear of corn and hair that looked like corn silk. Maya myth said the maize god would have his head cut off at harvest time. Then in the spring, he would be reborn during planting season. Corn's cycle of planting, harvesting, and replanting represents the cycle of life, death, and rebirth.

Native Mexicans avoided pellagra by boiling corn in limewater and making corn tortillas.

diet low in niacin can lead to a serious disease called pellagra. The first symptoms of the disease are reddened and thickened skin that looks similar to rose petals. Eventually, pellagra can lead to severe malnutrition and delusions.

The native people in the Americas knew how to prevent pellagra. They used a process the Aztec called *nixtamalization* that involved boiling and soaking the hard corn kernels in an alkali solution, such as limewater or lye made from wood ashes. Boiling and soaking made the tough outer hull easier to take off. After the hulls were removed, the kernels were then ground up, which released the niacin and improved the nutritional value of the corn. The result was called nixtamal or hominy.

Unfortunately, scientists did not understand the connection between corn and niacin until the 1900s. Pellagra remained a problem in Europe and Africa for approximately 200 years, especially among the poor.

COLONIAL AMERICA

As part of a varied diet or when processed into hominy, corn was an excellent food source. When colonists began settling in North America, corn helped them stay alive. In Jamestown, Virginia, in 1607, John Smith, the colony's first president, knew the only way for the colony to thrive was to learn how to grow native crops, such as corn.

Vampires

Scientists believe vampires might have really existed, not as mythological creatures that rise from the dead and feed off the living, but as real people who suffered from a disease. One culprit is pellagra. People with pellagra stopped eating because of sores in their throat and stomach, similar to how supposed vampires allegedly do not eat food. Pellagra sufferers also developed dementia and ended up in mental asylums, which might have increased the fear of people with the disease. Finally, because whole communities could get pellagra, some people might come down with the disease shortly after another person died from it. This may have made it seem like the dead person had returned to infect the living.

Pilgrims had a difficult time growing crops.

While other colonists dreamed of finding gold and heading back to Europe with their riches, Smith

learned native languages and wrote books about native plants. He believed corn was the only

gold worth having, especially since it could grow easily in the swampy Virginia land. In Plymouth,

Massachusetts, in 1621, the Pilgrims discovered the wheat they had brought with them across the Atlantic Ocean would not grow in the rocky New England soil. Only the native corn did well there.

By the late 1700s, the colonists had become extremely fond of corn. They used it to make hominy; succotash, or sweet corn and lima beans; johnnycake, a type of cornmeal flatbread; Boston brown bread; hush puppies; and other dishes. It was also cheaper and more abundant than other grains. A colonist could spend up to a week's wages buying a bushel of wheat. A bushel of corn, on the other hand, might cost only a few days' wages. Additionally, farmers discovered that corn yielded more grain than other crops. One ear of corn could produce approximately half a pound (0.23 kg) of grain. To make the same amount of grain from wheat or barley, a farmer would have to harvest approximately 100 ears of each.[1]

During this time, the word *corn* came into use as well. At first, it was a general word that referred to wheat, barley, and corn. Then colonists began calling corn *Indian corn* because of its relation to the native peoples. Eventually, the word was shortened to simply *corn* and was no longer used for other types of crops.

PIONEERS EXPAND WESTWARD

In the early 1800s, the United States was expanding south and west. In 1803, the Louisiana Purchase doubled the size of the United States and opened up new land for families who wanted to farm. The expansion came at a price for Native Americans, however. In the southern United States, white settlers pressured the US government to free up Native American land. So in 1823,

Farmers who traveled to the frontier first needed to clear their plots of trees and stumps.

the Supreme Court ruled Native American tribes could not own land, they could only occupy it. Then in 1830, President Andrew Jackson pushed the Indian Removal Act through Congress. This gave the president the power to negotiate treaties and force native people living east of the Mississippi River to move west. Some of the people moved voluntarily, but others resisted. Over a span of 28 years, the US government moved approximately 46,000 Indians from the southeastern United States to land west of the Mississippi, freeing up 25 million acres (10 million ha) of land for settlers.[2]

Settlers who moved to the Great Lakes region found rich, deep soil, and corn grew well there. However, settlers who moved to the Great Plains discovered more of a challenge. Much of the land was covered with sod that had a deep layer of tangled roots. Farmers had to chop through the roots before they could begin plowing. Even then, it was grueling work. Sometimes the plow animals died in their harnesses from the strain.

In 1837, a young man named John Deere created a new, more effective plow. Using German sawmill blades, his plow not only cut through the sod roots, it turned over the soil. As a result, his plow left neat furrows in the land that were ready for planting.

In 1862, President Abraham Lincoln signed the Homestead Act. This allowed families to obtain a plot of land for a small registration fee. The only requirement was that the homesteader had to be 21 years of age and the head of a family. Homesteaders had to agree to improve the land, which meant they had to farm it. With so much abundant and cheap land, many people moved to the

Free African Americans stand outside a homestead in Nicodemus, Kansas.

Great Plains. Sometimes new farm towns sprang up quickly, including one town in Kansas that consisted almost entirely of formerly enslaved African Americans.

By the end of the 1800s, corn production increased along with the number of farms. Corn became the dominant crop in the country, and the region where corn and soybeans were the main crops became known as the Corn Belt. Today, the Corn Belt includes the states of Indiana, Illinois, Iowa, Kansas, Minnesota, Missouri, Nebraska, and Wisconsin.

Nicodemus, Kansas

After the American Civil War (1861–1865), many African Americans were interested in looking for opportunities and prosperity away from the South. In September 1877, approximately 350 former slaves moved from Kentucky to Graham County, Kansas. Within the county, the town of Nicodemus quickly became the cultural center, and it grew rapidly throughout the 1880s as African Americans became farmers and business owners. By the early 1900s, Nicodemus boasted approximately 600 residents, but the town population declined after the Great Depression. Today it is a National Historic Site as the oldest and only standing black settlement west of the Mississippi River.

3 | A GROWING INDUSTRY

From the late 1800s until the present day, the corn industry grew from a simple crop to a multibillion dollar business. Along the way, there were many technological developments in transportation, farming equipment, seeds, and processing.

Early on, to get corn to market, farmers used boats or barges on rivers and streams. As towns and cities developed in the Midwest, farmers used roads, canals, and railroads to move their products. Chicago, Illinois, in particular, became a major hub for trading corn. Farmers shipped their corn by wagon or railroad car to giant grain elevators where it was stored in and around the city. When the corn was ready to be sold, it was poured into sacks with the farmer's name printed on them. The product was also weighed and inspected for quality.

To make sure the quality of the corn was consistent, the Chicago Board of Trade was established in 1848. This board created a grading system and used independent inspectors to assign grades. Having consistent quality standards allowed corn to be bought from anywhere in the country. For instance, a purchaser in New York could now

The Chicago Board of Trade helped Chicago become an agricultural center.

25

buy corn grown in Kansas and be confident in the quality of the product. Corn started to be sold as a commodity similar to a stock or bond. Not only did the board sell corn that was ready to be shipped, it also sold corn that had not been grown yet. This is called selling futures. The board could do this because independent inspectors could ensure the quality of the corn.

TECHNOLOGICAL IMPROVEMENTS

During the late 1800s and early 1900s, inventors came up with different machines to help farmers plow and harvest their corn. For instance, farmers could drag a V-shaped cutting sled to cut down stalks. They could also use a horse-drawn corn binder that would cut down stalks and bind them. However, none of the inventions were popular, and much work was still done by hand.

Everything changed in 1892 when John Froelich designed the first gasoline-powered traction machine, or tractor. Prior to this, traction machines were so heavy they compressed the soil. They were also powered by boilers, which often set crops on fire. Froelich's tractor was lighter and easier to use. In 1894, Froelich began a company to manufacture the tractors. Then in 1918, Deere & Company bought it and eventually became one of the world's largest tractor manufacturers.

With the invention of the tractor, farmers did not have to rely on horses or mules. Plus, plowing, planting, cultivating, and harvesting were easier with a tractor. Farms with tractors could do the same work with fewer workers. Unfortunately, the new tractors were expensive, and many farmers could not afford them. In 1917, automobile manufacturer Henry Ford designed his own version of the tractor and set the price much lower, making tractors available to more farmers.

Deere & Company is known for its trademark green and yellow equipment.

DEERE & COMPANY

In 1837, a young blacksmith named John Deere moved to Detour, Illinois, where he set up shop with a business partner. Located in farming country, Deere often found himself repairing the traditional wood and cast iron plows that farmers brought into his shop. He thought there must be a better way to make the plows so they could cut through the prairie soil without breaking. He tried different designs and sold ten plows in 1839. Five years later, Deere and his business partner were making approximately 1,000 plows a year.[1]

In 1847, Deere decided to strike off on his own, and he moved to Moline, Illinois. When he set up shop, he negotiated with a Pittsburgh, Pennsylvania, steel mill to make steel similar to English-made steel. And by 1857, he was producing 10,000 plows a year. [2] In 1868, the company was incorporated to Deere & Company with John as president. After that, the company began making other agricultural equipment. By 2012, its 175th anniversary, Deere & Company had net sales and revenues of $36 billion across many different industries.[3]

A corn head attaches to a combine, helping it turn out shelled corn.

Mechanical corn pickers also improved during the early 1900s. Pulled by tractors, the pickers broke the ears off the corn stalks and then peeled away the husks. However, many farmers could not afford corn pickers, especially during the Great Depression. The pickers were also difficult to set up and broke down frequently.

The combine solved these problems. Originally designed for wheat, this machine could both cut down and remove grain from the wheat plant. At first, combines were dragged behind tractors, but in the 1930s, a Canadian company developed the first self-propelled combine. Farmers could drive these combines instead of pulling them with tractors. Then in 1954, Deere & Company came up with a combine attachment specifically for harvesting corn. Called the "corn head," it could pick, husk, and shell corn in one operation.

With the arrival of combines came a new problem. Because farmers were now storing shelled corn, corncribs with large slats would not work anymore. The kernels would fall through the openings. Instead, farmers started using cylindrical steel grain bins. To keep the kernels from spoiling, the grain bins used drying systems that stirred the corn and allowed it to dry evenly.

Irrigation also improved in the mid-1900s. The old way of irrigating fields was to get water from a river or stream, or to pump it to the surface using a well. Farmers would then let water flow into ditches between rows of corn. From there, the farmers would either cut notches in the soil to let the water reach the individual plants or, as technology improved, use hoses to lead the water there. This was the gravity method of irrigation. One problem with the method, though, was that farmers had to grade their fields to make sure the slope was not too steep. If a field were too steep, the water could run off and accumulate only in the lowest parts of the field. In 1952, another system was invented. Called the pivot system, it could be used anywhere, even on steep land. The pivot system had a central water source with long sprayers that were attached to it like branches from a tree trunk. The branches rested on wheels and rotated around the central water source. This gave the fields an even, regular irrigation.

Equipment was not the only thing to improve. In the 1920s and 1930s, corn itself was bred into hybrid strains, in which a new plant is grown by breeding two different types of plants. The purpose of hybrids is to improve upon the original plant for traits such as greater yield and more uniformity. To reach the greater yield potential made possible by hybridization, industrial fertilizers were developed to help corn grow. Also, during World War II (1939–1945), the United

States produced massive amounts of ammonia to use in explosives. Ammonia is rich in nitrogen, an excellent plant fertilizer. After the war, the United States' vast ammonia production was repurposed to help farmers increase crop yields. Corn yields increased dramatically after these developments. Farmers were able to grow more corn on the same acreage of land.

Corn Yield

Corn yield rose throughout the second half of the 1900s due to advancements in hybridization and fertilization.

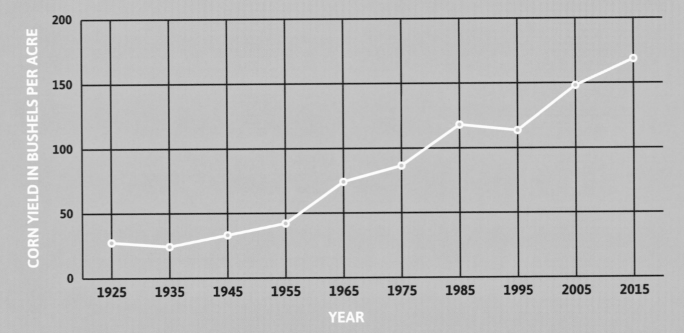

Corn Whiskey

One way farmers got their corn to market was turning it into whiskey, which would not go bad. In Virginia in 1620, corn whiskey became a popular drink for colonists. By the mid-1800s, thousands of gallons of whiskey were being produced in distilleries. So much whiskey was made in the Midwest that Peoria, Illinois, became known as the Whiskey Capital of the World. However, the Eighteenth Amendment, which was passed in 1920, made the manufacture, sale, and transportation of alcohol illegal. This greatly reduced the amount of whiskey sold in the United States. After Prohibition was repealed in 1933, whiskey production resumed at a reduced level.

GETTING CORN TO MARKET

Historically, after corn was harvested, farm families would use some of the corn for themselves and some as feed for their farm animals. But farmers also wanted to make money with their crops, so they had to sell the corn before it could spoil. One way of getting corn to market was by feeding it to livestock. Farmers discovered that many animals readily ate corn, and corn provided animals with almost all of their nutritional needs. Also, animals could eat the entire corn plant. In the 1800s, when large corn-fed herds of pigs were sent to market, they were referred to as "cornfields with legs."[4]

In the mid-1800s, new canning technology allowed sweet corn to be sold in stores months after it was harvested. And in the late 1800s, popcorn became a popular snack, giving corn farmers another way to earn money. Canned corn increased in popularity, and in 1910 more than 13 million cans of corn were sold. In the 1940s, the company Birds Eye developed a way to rapidly freeze corn and other vegetables, which provided another way for farmers to get corn to market.

PROCESSING CORN

In the 1800s, many farmers lived far from towns and cities, so they had to grind up the corn themselves. To do this, they used a quern, or hand mill. Villages sprang up near rivers, along with waterwheels. Waterwheels were used to turn giant stones, which would grind the corn. Waterwheels and grindstones were housed in large buildings called gristmills.

In 1842, Thomas Kingsford, an employee at William Colgate & Company, came up with a way to separate the starch from the rest of the corn kernel. He used a new process called wet milling, which soaked the kernels in a solution before they were ground up. Wet milling made it easier to isolate the starch, which was then turned into laundry starch. In 1846, Kingsford started his own starch company, and by 1880 he was making 35 short tons (31.7 metric tons) of cornstarch per day.[5] But starch was not just used for laundry. After 1850, it was used to thicken sauces and make desserts.

Popcorn

In the 1800s, most popcorn was grown in home gardens. Families experimented with different ways to pop it without burning the kernels. Then in 1893, Charles Cretors invented a machine that would not only pop the popcorn, it would salt and butter it. Arranged on a beautiful cart that could be wheeled from place to place, Cretors's invention helped popcorn become a new industry. In 1895, the Rueckheim brothers experimented with sweet coatings for popcorn and mixed them with peanuts. The result was Cracker Jack, which became a classic snack in the United States. With this new popcorn market opening up, farmers started growing, shelling, and selling popcorn to stores. Sales took off in the early to mid-1900s, especially when motion pictures and then television became popular. Today, almost all popcorn is grown in the Midwest. Nebraska alone grows approximately 295 million pounds (134 million kg) of shelled popcorn per year.[6]

An 1885 advertisement for Kingsford's Oswego Starch shows its use in ironing clothing.

Wet milling led to the development of other corn products. In 1866, cornstarch was further processed into glucose, a type of sugar made from corn. After even more refinement, an even sweeter product called high-fructose corn syrup (HFCS) was developed. HFCS became the main sweetener of soft drinks and many sweet foods.

In the late 1800s, scientists discovered how to remove the oil from the corn kernel. Not only could corn oil now be used in cooking, it was used to help make a myriad of other products, such as soap, paint, varnish, and other items.

In the late 1800s and early 1900s, other ways of processing corn became popular. In Battle Creek, Michigan, two companies began marketing dry cereals as a new breakfast food. They created corn flakes by cooking and drying corn before crushing the mixture between two cylinders to form flakes. One example of a corn-based breakfast cereal is Kellogg's Corn Flakes.

In the 1930s, Charles Elmer Doolin began a business that involved pounding corn into a paste, forming it into shapes, and frying it. This is similar to how Native Americans had cooked tortillas for thousands of years. Doolin, however, created a snack food called "Fritos" with the method. He started giving them to customers at his restaurant in Anaheim, California. Eventually, he sold Fritos and Doritos—which are made through a similar process—throughout the country.

Kellogg's Corn Flakes

In 1876, Dr. John Harvey Kellogg was a superintendent of a health facility in Battle Creek, Michigan. He believed he could improve the health of his patients if he fed them whole grains. Along with his younger brother, Kellogg developed the first cornflakes and rice flakes. This process involves cooking the corn under pressure, drying it, and then flattening it into flakes. In 1900, the Kellogg brothers created their own cereal company. Six years later, Will Kellogg bought out his brother and renamed the company the Kellogg Toasted Corn Flake Company. Because the company started making cereals out of grains other than corn, in 1922 the name was changed to the Kellogg Company.

ETHANOL

In addition to food products, corn plants can be processed into industrial uses. Corn stalks can be used to make paper. Corn resins can be turned into watches. Corn husks and stalks can be made into skateboards. And corn kernels can be distilled into ethanol fuel.

Made from sugary crops such as corn, barley, and sugarcane, ethanol is a clear, colorless alcohol. In the 1850s, people used ethanol to light lanterns. But during the American Civil War (1861–1865), the government taxed all alcohol to raise money for the war. This included ethanol, so people switched to kerosene as a fuel source. When the tax was repealed in 1906, ethanol use increased again. Henry Ford even designed his Model T automobile to run on a combination of gasoline and ethanol.

Because of Prohibition and the abundance of cheap oil, ethanol never took off in the mid-1900s. However, in the 1970s, oil prices rose dramatically, and people wanted to save money. One solution was to add ethanol to gasoline. Since ethanol can be made by simply growing more corn, it is considered a renewable fuel. Gasoline, on the other hand, is made from crude oil, a nonrenewable fossil fuel. In 2005, Congress passed the Renewable Fuel Standard. This act says manufacturers had to use a certain amount of renewable fuels, including ethanol. In 2014, the United Stated added approximately 13 billion gallons (49 billion L) of ethanol to gasoline.[7]

4 | GROWING AND HARVESTING CORN

In the corn industry, many different businesses contribute to the success of farmers. Seed companies such as Monsanto and DuPont provide the corn seeds. Equipment manufacturers such as Deere & Company, Case IH, New Holland, and AGCO provide tractors, combines, planters, and all the equipment needed to plant and grow corn. Crop protection companies including Bayer, Syngenta, and Dow AgroSciences make pesticides, fungicides, and herbicides that prevent insects, fungi, and weeds from damaging crops. Fertilizer companies such as the Potash Corporation, the Mosaic Company, and Koch Fertilizer help the soil have the proper nutrients. And lenders such as the Farm Credit System and Wells Fargo provide loans to farmers so they can buy their first farm or the expensive equipment and material needed to run it.

SEEDS

Choosing seeds is the first step in growing corn, and there are three types of seeds farmers can buy: open-pollinated, hybrid, and genetically modified. In all corn, pollen grains are transferred from the

Farmers must make informed decisions about which seeds are best for them.

Pioneer offers dozens of hybrid seed options.

PIONEER HI-BRED

In the early 1900s, farmers believed the best-looking ears of corn would produce the best corn yield. They even competed in competitions for the prettiest ears of corn and used the winning seeds for the next year's crop. However, 16-year-old Henry Wallace questioned this practice. He conducted an experiment in which he grew two corn plants: one from the seeds of an ugly ear and one from the seeds from a pretty ear. He then compared the resulting plants. The ugly ear ended up producing more corn than the pretty ear.

In 1926, Wallace founded a corn seed company with his brother. Hi-Bred Corn Company—later known as Pioneer Hi-Bred Corn Company—became the first company devoted to hybrid corn. The company's first hybrid crop was hand planted and handpicked on 40 acres (16 ha) of land. Soon Pioneer's corn was winning competitions and beating open-pollinated corn. Wallace went on to become US secretary of agriculture and vice president. His company expanded. Today it supplies seeds in more than 90 countries.[1]

male structure of one plant to female structures of another. The tassel at the top of the plant is the male structure, and the female structure consists of the ears on the stalks, which contain rows of ovules. When pollen lands on the ovules, they turn into kernels, which are the corn seeds.

Open-pollinated seeds occur when pollen from one corn plant attaches to the ovules of another, genetically different plant. The resulting seed is a mix of the two plants' genetic makeup. While some farmers use open-pollinated seeds, most use hybrid seeds. With hybrid seeds, each parent plant is created by breeding plants that are genetically similar. This gives the seeds uniform traits. Seeds from two different lines are grown so the plants can cross-pollinate. The resulting seeds are a hybrid of both plants, called an F1 hybrid. To control pollination in a hybrid, a breeder places a bag over the tassel to trap the falling pollen. Then the bag is moved over the ears for pollination.

While F1 hybrids are bred for some traits, they may not carry or exhibit other desirable traits. For example, many F1 hybrids are not tolerant to cold weather, or they are at an increased risk of insect damage. They may require heavy use of pesticides, herbicides, and fertilizers to compensate for the weaknesses of being an F1 hybrid. In addition, if F1 hybrids are allowed to cross-pollinate, the resulting seeds will not be uniform and may be inferior in some ways. This means farmers have to buy new seeds each time they plant.

Another type of seed is called a genetically modified organism (GMO). In GMO corn plants the genetic code of one or both of the parent plants has been altered by inserting new genetic

Researchers grow GMO corn under a roof to test its resistance to drought.

sequences. These additions allow the plant to have traits not usually found in corn, such as proteins that are toxic to insects or proteins that protect the plant from herbicides. In the 1960s and 1970s, scientists started modifying foods on a molecular and cellular level. The first GMO product was created in 1993 when the US Food and Drug Administration approved a growth hormone for dairy cows that increases their milk production. The following year, a tomato was genetically modified to have a longer shelf life. Since then, many more GMO products have been developed, including corn seeds. One GMO corn seed produces a crop that creates its own pesticides. Another produces a crop that stays safe when certain herbicides are sprayed around it to kill weeds.

GMO seeds can be more tolerant to herbicides and pesticides, and they can help plants endure environmental stresses better, such as droughts. In addition, with some genetically modified corn, farmers see higher corn yields, and the farmers can plant corn closer together to get more corn on the same amount of land. Some genetically modified corn can also be grown in a continuous cycle on the same field.

SOIL NUTRIENTS AND CROP PROTECTION

As corn roots grow, they provide a place for fungi to grow. The fungi feed off the sugars the corn plant provides through photosynthesis. In turn, the fungi give the corn nutrients and water from the soil. These nutrients include nitrogen, phosphorus, potassium, sulfur, and calcium. They also include several trace elements, such as copper, zinc, and iron that corn needs in smaller quantities. To make sure the proper nutrients are in the soil, farmers test both the soil and the leaves of the plant.

Monsanto

In 1982, Monsanto became the first company to genetically modify a plant cell, but the company did not begin in agriculture. Founded in 1901 by John F. Queeny, Monsanto started out making saccharin, an artificial sweetener. Soon after, Queeny added caffeine and vanilla to the lineup, and Coca-Cola became one of the company's main customers. In 1945, the company created its first agriculture chemicals, and by the 1960s Monsanto was a leading herbicide producer. In 1981, biotechnology became the company's main focus, and by the late 1990s, the company was selling a variety of genetically modified seeds.

Crop rotation is one way of ensuring the soil has the proper nutrients. During crop rotation, different crops are planted in the same field in a specific order. Because grass crops such as corn cannot produce their own nitrogen in the soil, they need something else to provide nitrogen. This could come from fertilizer

Corn, right, and soybeans, left, are often grown in rotation.

or from a legume, such as soybean. Both of these add nitrogen to the soil. Typical crop rotations might be a two-year rotation of corn and soybean or a four-year rotation of soybean, corn, alfalfa, and wheat. Crop rotation can add flavor to sweet corn, and some canneries require farmers to rotate their sweet corn crops with other plants.

Most large-scale farmers turn to artificial fertilizers to add missing nutrients to the soil. Fertilizer can be sold as individual chemicals or as a mixture of two or more chemicals, depending on the needs of the farmer. Corn uses approximately half of all the fertilizer used in the United States with approximately 1.5 to 2 pounds (0.7–0.9 kg) of fertilizer needed per bushel of corn.[2]

Growing Corn Seeds

Corn grows best in warm, deep soil that is well aerated, meaning it has lots of pockets in which air can circulate. Corn also needs water and fertilizer. Since the roots of a corn plant can grow up to six feet (1.8 m) long, it is important for the soil to be tilled properly both before and after planting. Proper tilling removes weeds from the seedbed. It chops up the hard, compacted soil that can block roots, and it protects the soil from erosion due to wind or rain. Finally, as old, dried corn material or cover crop is chopped up during tilling, it allows this material to be evenly distributed into the soil, which increases the organic material in the soil.

Roundup

In 1970, Monsanto chemist John Franz began studying two water-softening chemicals that showed signs of being herbicides. Franz applied the chemicals to plants and watched how the plants responded. From this, he was able to create a new chemical called glyphosate that was a powerful herbicide. Other herbicides at that time were designed to kill specific weeds. Glyphosate, however, could kill every plant that it touched. And because Monsanto developed genetically modified corn that can resist glyphosate, farmers could spray it around their crops, and all the weeds would die but not the corn. With Roundup, farmers did not have to till to control weeds. Glyphosate was deemed to be safer for the environment than other herbicides. In 1974, Monsanto named it Roundup, and today it is one of the world's best-selling herbicides.[3]

In addition to maintaining fertile soil, farmers must monitor corn crops for diseases that affect their roots, stalks, and leaves, such as root and stalk rot or leaf blights. Farmers must also watch for nematodes, tiny worms that damage plants' roots. Other insects and weeds can also cause problems. Farmers use different chemicals to help mitigate the effects of pests and diseases. Sometimes, seeds are treated with chemicals ahead of time to prevent problems from arising later on. One company, Monsanto, even created a genetically modified seed that would be resistant to Roundup, an herbicide the company created. Farmers buy Monsanto's seeds and herbicide to get the benefits from each.

HARVESTING CORN

As corn grows, it goes through several stages. When corn is still green, the kernels are juicy and sweet. Called the milk stage, sweet corn is harvested at this time, and the ears of the corn are picked whole with the husks still on them.

Farmers can hire crop consultants to examine corn for signs of disease.

Dent corn, on the other hand, goes through two more stages. After the milk stage, the kernel becomes doughier because the sugars in the kernel turn to starch. When the kernels reach maturity, they develop a black layer at their tips. This occurs about a month after sweet corn has matured. However, the moisture content of the dent kernels at the black-layer stage is approximately 35 percent. Farmers prefer letting their corn stay on the stalk until the moisture content falls to approximately 20 percent, because it is easier and less costly to store corn that contains less moisture.

Farmers pay fees to store their corn crop off-site.

Once corn reaches the right level of moisture, it is harvested and transferred to a storage elevator, where it is dried to prevent mold and rot. The goal is to get corn to 15.5 percent moisture content.[4] That is the level at which grain buyers will purchase the corn. Some farmers own their own storage elevators and dry their own corn, but others pay to have it dried and stored off-site.

After the corn is dried, it is inspected and graded. According to the United States Department of Agriculture (USDA), "corn" is defined as shelled dent or flint corn composed of at least 50 percent whole kernels.[5] Once the grain meets that requirement, inspectors take samples from either a barge, truck, railroad car, or other container. They determine the class of the corn, which can be either yellow, white, or a mixture of both, and test the moisture content. After that, they inspect the corn, taking into consideration the amount of broken corn, the weight of the corn, and the amount of foreign materials in the corn.

Finally, inspectors assign a grade from one to five, with one being the highest quality. US No. 1 weighs the most per bushel and has the fewest damaged kernels and foreign material. US No. 5 weighs the least per bushel and has the most damaged kernels and foreign material. Corn that is below a grade 5 is called US Sample Grade.

5 | PROCESSING CORN

After a corn crop is harvested and stored, it is either sold as livestock feed or sold to a processing plant. There are two different ways to process corn: wet milling and dry milling. Wet milling produces items such as corn oil, cornstarch, and corn syrup. Dry milling produces cereal, grits, cornmeal, and other food items. Both kinds of processing end up with coproducts, or remains that become animal feed. Dry-milling companies include Didion Milling, Agricor, and Bunge. Cargill and ADM have both wet and dry processing plants.

WET MILLING

Dent corn is used for most wet-milled corn products in the United States. After the corn is inspected and cleaned, it is poured into tanks and soaked. The kernel absorbs a lot of the water and increases in size. Acid in the water helps release the kernels' starch.

Once the corn has soaked, it goes through a coarse grinder, which leaves the grain fairly large and rough. This breaks the germ loose from the rest of the kernel. What is left is a slurry of ground kernels: fiber, starch, protein, and germ, all suspended in water. Any

Unprocessed corn can be used to make livestock feed.

ADM's processing plant in Illinois is the largest corn wet mill in the world.

ADM

In 1902, John W. Daniels began a company to process flaxseed into linseed oil. Linseed oil can be used as a cooking oil or in the production of paints, inks, and varnishes. A year later, George Archer became a partner, and the company was renamed to Archer-Daniels Linseed Company. For the next 20 years, they continued to process flaxseed, but profits were low. In 1923, they bought the Midland Linseed Products Company and changed the name to Archer Daniels Midland Company, or ADM. Throughout the 1900s, Daniels and Archer expanded the company and explored ways of using plant material in new and innovative ways, such as turning oil into soaps, medications, brake fluids, and other chemicals. In 1971, the company bought a corn sweetener company, and in the 1980s, it began producing ethanol and high-fructose corn syrup. It also runs wet- and dry-milling plants. Today, ADM is a global food processing company, and in 2014 the company had a revenue of $81.2 billion.[1]

excess water is drained and sent to use in animal feeds, because it contains a lot of the nutrients from the corn. Next, the slurry is sent to a machine that spins at a super high speed. This allows the lighter germs to slip out. The germs are then processed to extract their oil. Since approximately 85 percent of the germ is oil, most of it becomes corn oil. This oil can be used as cooking oil or as an ingredient in margarine. The rest of the germ is turned into animal feed.

Now that the germs and their oil are gone from the slurry, it needs to be ground again. This time, the slurry goes through a fine grind. The purpose is to release the starch and gluten from the fiber. Then, the slurry passes through a screen that filters out the fiber. This fiber is used for animal feed.

The remaining slurry consists of just two parts of the kernel: starch and gluten. The mixture is sent to separators that spin out the gluten. The remaining starch slurry is mixed with water and washed up to 14 times, to make sure all of the gluten is gone. Once the purity of the cornstarch reaches 99.5 percent, the process is complete.[2] Some of the cornstarch is sold to other companies as unmodified cornstarch. Companies use this dry

Cornstarch

When added to water and gradually heated, starch increases in size and thickens any liquid it is mixed into. This makes cornstarch a useful food additive for puddings, gravies, sauces, and pie fillings. Cornstarch can also be made into a paste and used with food or as a coating for paper. If the starch paste is cooled, it forms a gel. This gel can be mixed in puddings, salad dressings, and some adhesives. If cornstarch paste is spread on smooth surfaces, it creates a strong adhesive and can be used in making textiles, corrugated cardboard, and paper.

white powder to make many different products. Yet despite cornstarch's many uses, the majority of cornstarch is processed even more to make corn syrup.

To transform cornstarch into corn syrup, it is mixed with acids or enzymes, which turn the starch into glucose, or sugar. The extent to which the cornstarch is converted to glucose depends on the type of syrup being made. Once the desired sweetness is reached, the excess water is removed, and only corn syrup remains. Corn syrup can be sold as is, or it can be sent to a fermentation plant to be turned into alcohol. Corn syrup can also be processed even more to make high-fructose corn syrup (HFCS).

HIGH-FRUCTOSE CORN SYRUP

Introduced in the 1970s, HFCS is a sweetener similar to table sugar in chemical composition. The advantage of HFCS over table sugar is that HFCS is stable in acidic foods and beverages. Because it is a liquid, it can also be transferred more easily than granular sugar from trucks to storage facilities. The supply of HFCS is also more dependable than sugar, where price and availability can be an issue. For these reasons, the food industry has embraced HFCS, and today HFCS is used in many products, such as sodas, fruit-flavored beverages, bread, yogurt, honey-roasted peanuts, ketchup, canned fruits, and preserves.

There is some controversy surrounding HFCS, however. Because of rising obesity rates in the United States, critics wonder if HFCS is to blame. They want to know if our bodies process HFCS differently than table sugar. But no evidence has been found to support a difference, and experts

High-fructose corn syrup is often used in soda because it is more stable than sugar.

Corn kernels are processed to remove dirt and debris.

say that too much of any sugar, not just HFCS, can increase calories in a person's diet.[3]

DRY MILLING

Another way of processing corn is through dry milling. Unlike wet milling, which requires a large investment in equipment and money, dry milling is less expensive and does not need as large of a capital investment. However, dry milling is not as versatile as wet milling, and it cannot make as wide a variety of products. Ethanol and cornmeal are primarily made by dry milling. Companies such as General Mills use dry-milled corn for their food products.

The first step in dry milling is to clean the corn. At this time, broken pieces of corn as well as dust, dirt, and other debris are separated out. Once the corn is clean, it is brought up to a moisture level of 20 percent.[4] This makes it easier to take out every part of the kernel except for the large, starchy part, or endosperm. Next, the corn is sent to a machine called a "degerminator" that separates out the germs. The remaining endosperm is cooled and sifted. From there, it continues on to be processed in grinding tables, roller mills, and sifters, depending on how fine the end product needs to be.

The coarsest products become flaking grits, which are used to make cornflake cereal. Cornmeal, which is less coarse than flaking grits, is used to make corn bread, muffins, fritters, and hush puppies. If the cornmeal is ground even finer, it goes into products such as cereals, pizzas, and English muffins. The cornmeal with the finest grind becomes corn flour, and it is used in

A worker at a dry mill in Germany examines the ground grain.

dry bakery mixes, muffins, donuts, breading, baby foods, and even meat products.

Meanwhile, the remaining germ goes through a second degerminator to separate the bran from the germ. Eventually, the processed germ is turned into various products, such as corn oil, hominy, grits, and flour.

Jiffy Mix

In the 1920s, Mabel White Holmes's sons invited a friend over for lunch. The young boy brought a brown paper sack with him. When he opened it, Holmes was dismayed to discover a rock-hard biscuit inside. It was clear that an inexperienced baker had made the biscuit, and Holmes wondered if she could help. Her husband ran the Chelsea Milling Company in Chelsea, Michigan, so in 1930, Holmes convinced him to produce her biscuit mix in his mill. She named it Jiffy Mix because a person can bake it up in a jiffy. The business expanded to include corn muffins, cakes, frostings, piecrusts, and pizza doughs. When demand is highest, from September to January, Jiffy makes approximately 1.6 million boxes of its mixes per day.[5]

6 | ETHANOL

Ethanol is the most common product created through the dry-milling process. Almost all ethanol made in the United States comes from corn, and approximately 90 percent of it is made through dry milling.[1]

To make ethanol, corn kernels are first ground in a hammer mill into fine flour. Next, water and enzymes are added. These additions turn the cornmeal into simple sugar. Yeast is added to make the mixture ferment. The fermentation process breaks down the simple sugar into carbon dioxide and alcohol. The resulting mixture is distilled until it is 100 percent ethyl alcohol, or ethanol. Before the ethanol is shipped, gasoline is added. This is to make the ethanol unfit for human consumption, so it cannot be taxed or used to make alcoholic beverages.

Throughout the process, ethanol by-products are not thrown out. The carbon dioxide from fermentation is sold to other businesses, such as bottling companies and dry-ice companies. And the remaining solids from the mash are processed further and turned into animal feed.

Ethanol is transported in sanitized shipping containers.

Ethanol Jobs

In 2011, 40 percent of the corn grown in the United States went to ethanol production. This is 5 billion bushels of corn grown solely for ethanol.[5] Such a large industry brings jobs and opportunities to many people. In 2011, the ethanol industry employed 90,200 workers directly and 311,400 workers indirectly in areas such as engineering, accounting, and chemistry. For instance, in Hugoton, Kansas, when Abengoa Bioenergy built a new ethanol plant, it employed 300 people during construction. After the plant became operational, it employed approximately 65 people with full-time jobs.[6]

A FUEL ADDITIVE

Ethanol's main use is as an additive to fuel. More than 96 percent of all gasoline in the United States includes ethanol.[2] But ethanol is added to gasoline in varying amounts. A common mixture is called E10, which is 10 percent ethanol and 90 percent gasoline. If the blend is 15 percent ethanol and 85 percent gasoline, it's called E15. An even greater amount of ethanol is available in the E85 mixture. This blend has anywhere from 51 to 83 percent ethanol, depending on where and when the fuel is produced.[3]

Almost all vehicles already use E10, but not many vehicles use E15 or E85 yet. In 2015, most of the new vehicles sold in the United States were made with E15 fuel in mind. Experts say that it may take another ten years to convert all vehicles on the road to the higher ethanol amount.[4] In 2016, approximately 20 percent of vehicles could operate on the E15 fuel. As for the E85 fuel, only certain vehicles could use it. They are called flexible fuel vehicles (FFVs). They require modifications to the fuel components and control systems. Alcohol in such high amounts can be corrosive and harmful to standard car parts, so they require different materials.

There are several benefits to adding ethanol to gasoline. One is that it may lower greenhouse gas emissions. It also adds octane to gasoline, which reduces engine knocking and improves engine performance. Another benefit of ethanol is it can decrease the United States' dependence on foreign oil. Petroleum imports decreased from 60 percent in 2005 to approximately 25 percent in 2015.[7] Only some of that decrease was due to ethanol, but it did aid in the change. According to the Renewable Fuels Association, US imports of petroleum would have been 32 percent in 2015 without ethanol.[8] Finally, E85 ethanol is less expensive than E10 gasoline, and may provide greater performance in E85 vehicles. Unfortunately, E85 fuel has a 15 to 27 percent lower fuel economy than regular gasoline.[9] Fuel economy is the amount of fuel it takes to run a vehicle. The less fuel it takes, the more economical it is.

FFVs

Flexible fuel vehicles look like regular cars. Other than a yellow fuel cap, drivers might not even know they have one. The difference is that FFVs are made to run on fuel that ranges anywhere from E10 to E85. As of 2016, more than 50 models were available to accommodate E85 fuel. These vehicles include the Audi Quattro, Buick LaCrosse, Chevrolet Impala, Chevrolet Suburban, Chrysler Town & Country, Dodge Durango, Ford Explorer, and Ford Focus, as well as vehicles from GMC, Jeep, Mercedes, Nissan, and Toyota. E85 is available at more than 2,700 fueling stations across the country.[10]

Controversy remains over whether using ethanol in cars lowers greenhouse gas emissions.

ETHANOL CONTROVERSY

There are several controversies associated with ethanol. One is that making ethanol might not decrease greenhouse gas emissions as compared to petroleum. Some environmental groups say plowing up land that has not been used for farming to make corn for fuel is an inefficient way to cut down on greenhouse gas emissions. Carbon is released from the soil after it is plowed, and fuel is burned to harvest corn and process it for ethanol. All of these actions lead to greater greenhouse gas emissions.

To compare ethanol and gasoline, it is important to look at the life cycle of both fuels. A life cycle includes all of the steps it takes to make each product. For ethanol, there is the energy it takes to grow the corn, transport it to a plant, make the ethanol, distribute it to gas companies, and use the fuel in vehicles. With petroleum, its life cycle includes drilling for oil, transporting it to a refinery, converting it to gasoline, distributing it, and using it in vehicles. In 2012, the Argonne National Laboratory did a study on the life cycles of ethanol and gasoline. It found ethanol reduced greenhouse gas emissions by 19 to 52 percent compared to gasoline, depending on how much energy is used to make the ethanol.[11] If natural gas is used in the process, then the greenhouse gas reduction is 28 percent. However, if coal is used, then the reduction might not be realized. A 2014 study from the Congressional Budget Office came up with a different result. It determined that

Ethanol Growth

When the Renewable Fuel Standard was passed in 2005, Congress declared that vehicles should operate with a minimum percent of renewable fuel in gasoline. Because of corn's abundance and its ability to be converted into ethanol, corn production increased dramatically. So did construction of ethanol plants. Since it is less costly for a plant to be near its source of corn, most of the ethanol plants are located in the Midwest too. More than 400 ethanol facilities are operating in the United States as of January 2016, with another three under construction. In 2015, these refineries produced 14.7 billion gallons (55.6 million L) of fuel in 29 states.[12]

ethanol only had a small effect on reducing greenhouse gases.[13] As other studies are underway, the effects of ethanol on greenhouse gases are still being determined.

Another controversy surrounding ethanol is whether it reduces fuel economy in vehicles. Not only would this cost drivers more money in fuel, it would be bad for the environment because more gasoline would be burned. It is true that burning ethanol creates less energy than gasoline. One gallon (3.8 L) of pure ethanol creates approximately 76,000 Btus while one gallon (3.8 L) of gasoline creates approximately 112,000 Btus. If drivers were to use E85 fuel, they would notice their fuel economy go down approximately 25 percent. But for most drivers who use E10 or E15, they would not see a difference.[14]

Finally, many people argue that the land used to grow corn for ethanol could be used to grow corn as food. However, growing corn has become more and more efficient over the years, which means the same amount of land can grow more corn than ever before. In 2000, US farms produced 137 bushels per acre. In 2015, they produced 169 bushels per acre.[15] In addition, ethanol uses only approximately 3 percent of the world's grain supplies.[16]

7 | ENVIRONMENTAL ISSUES

With so much corn being grown in the United States, it is bound to have an effect on the environment. Irrigation can deplete water supplies while excess fertilizer can contaminate these same sources. In addition, the corn industry not only contributes to climate change, it is affected by it.

IRRIGATION

Water from irrigation is an environmental issue for many farmers. They have to worry about surface evaporation and about depleting aquifers used as a source for irrigation. Most corn farmers get their water from rainfall, but those who do rely on irrigation use a lot of it. Even though corn is relatively efficient in its use of water, overall, it draws more water from irrigation than any other crop grown in the United States. Corn uses approximately 17 percent of all agricultural water. This is because corn production has risen over the past 20 years, causing irrigation use to rise as well.[1]

One way irrigation efficiency can be improved is by turning to the pivot irrigation system rather than surface irrigation methods such as the flood or furrow systems. In the flood system,

Farmers in particularly dry areas rely on irrigation to maintain good yields.

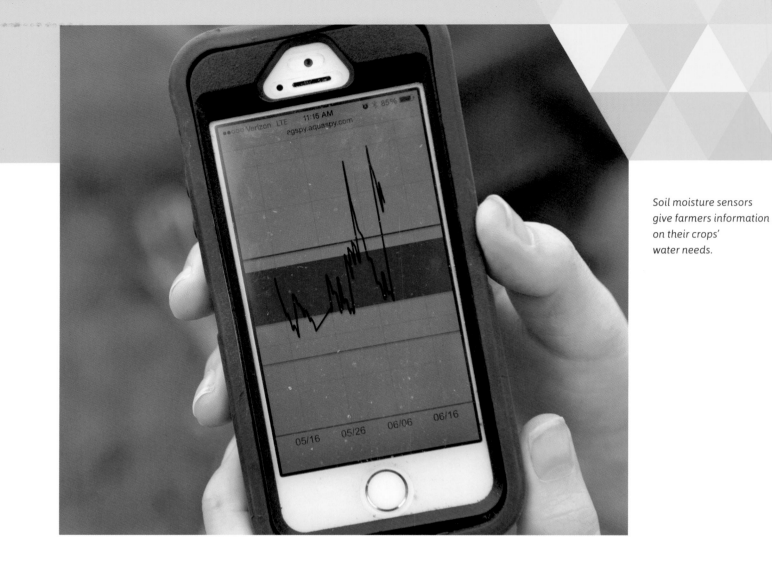

Soil moisture sensors give farmers information on their crops' water needs.

water floods an entire field from one end to the other. In the furrow system, the water runs down the furrows between plants. In the pivot system, water is applied more directly to plants. Forms of drip irrigation are also more efficient. In these systems, water is dripped at a low rate onto the soil very close to the plants. This method is also called trickle irrigation.

Soil-moisture monitors and other new technologies can tell farmers how much to irrigate based on the unique plant and soil characteristics and weather patterns associated with their crops. Because the newest irrigation technologies are expensive, though, most farmers do not yet use them.

Extended crop rotations can also reduce water use. In this method, crops are rotated every three years instead of every other year. This improves the health of the soil, so less water and fertilizer are needed. The use of cover crops is another technique in which plants that are grown to protect the soil from erosion, conserve water, and filter out pollution. Cover crops are non-commodity crops planted to protect soil. Corn planted after a year of a cover crop can have an increased yield, especially for areas that have been hit by a drought. Finally, drought-resistant seeds show promise of being able to reduce irrigation. Monsanto, DuPont, and Syngenta are all developing these seeds.

No-Till Farming

Some farmers reduce their use of irrigation water by employing different planting techniques. One of these techniques is called the no-till method. In this method, old crop material is not plowed under. Instead, seeds are pushed directly through old crop material. The material acts like mulch to protect the soil and conserve water. This type of tillage also reduces erosion and fertilizer runoff. However, the downside to the no-till method is that it requires specialized seeding equipment. Plus, extra moisture in the soil could lead to fungal diseases, and since weeds are not broken up with a plow, farmers may have to use extra herbicides to kill weeds.

The USDA funds research on the most effective forms of irrigation, including underground drip irrigation.

Federal, state, and local authorities are also getting involved to help conserve water. On the federal level, the USDA's Natural Resources Conservation Service (NRCS) has partnered with local governments to help reduce aquifer use. At the state level, Kansas passed legislation in 2012 encouraging farmers to use less water during wetter years so they can use more water during drier years.

FERTILIZER

Corn uses more fertilizer per acre than any other major crop. In 2013, corn used 140 pounds per acre (157 kg/ha) of nitrogen while wheat used 65 pounds per acre (73 kg/ha) and soy used just 16 pounds per acre (18 kg/ha). In fact, corn takes in more than half of all the fertilizer used on crops in the United States.[2]

Grasses can filter out fertilizers and keep them from harming the environment. However, the high demand for corn often means natural filters such as grasses have been removed to make room for more crops. And farmers use fewer cover crops, which could absorb more of the fertilizer. Corn is unique in that so much of it is grown as animal feed. When feed corn is harvested, the entire corn plant is removed and shredded. This leaves little of it on the ground, which can lead to soil erosion. As good topsoil erodes away, farmers have to use more fertilizer the next time they plant their crops.

Meet David Brandt

David Brandt is a corn and soybean farmer in rural Ohio. With 1,200 acres (486 ha) of land, he does not use conventional farming methods. Instead of letting his field remain bare as the neighboring farmers do, he plants cover crops. More than 14 different plants, including hairy vetch, rye, and radishes, completely cover the soil to feed the microbes that live in it. "We're trying to mimic Mother Nature," he says.[3] Then in the spring, he lets the crops rot. And instead of tilling the soil the conventional way, Brandt uses the no-till method. He does not want to disturb soil nutrients or microbes. Plus, no-tilling helps prevent erosion and protects it from flooding. In addition, Brandt adds a third crop to his rotation—wheat—to disrupt weeds and pests. All of these methods cut down on fertilizer, herbicides, and other chemicals. Brandt's crops benefit from his methods. His farm often produces higher-than-average yields in his county.

When farmers use too much fertilizer, additional environmental problems can arise. The three main ingredients of fertilizer are nitrogen, potassium, and phosphate. If there is too much nitrogen or phosphorous in a water system, then too much algae can grow. In turn, this depletes the oxygen in the water, which can cause problems or death for marine life. Currently, 80 percent of corn and soybean farms are located in the region where runoff ends up in the Mississippi River.[4] This region

Sources of Nitrogen and Phosphorus Entering the Gulf of Mexico

As shown in the charts below, runoff from land dedicated to corn and soybean crops is responsible for more than half of the nitrogen and a quarter of the phosphorus entering the Gulf of Mexico each year.

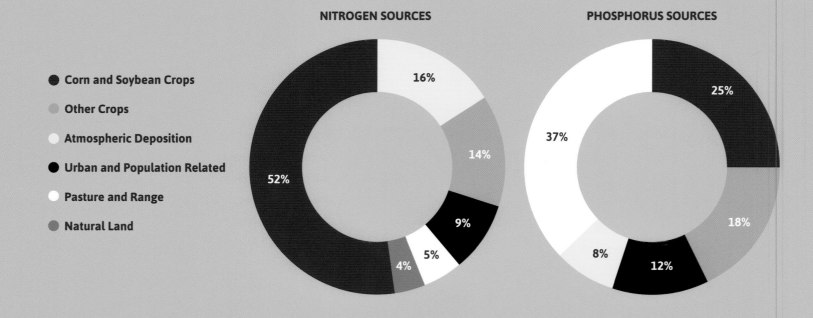

NITROGEN SOURCES

PHOSPHORUS SOURCES

- ● Corn and Soybean Crops
- ○ Other Crops
- ○ Atmospheric Deposition
- ● Urban and Population Related
- ○ Pasture and Range
- ● Natural Land

Nitrogen Sources: 16%, 14%, 9%, 5%, 4%, 52%

Phosphorus Sources: 25%, 18%, 12%, 8%, 37%

Farmers can receive money for allowing a barrier of natural vegetation to grow between crops and bodies of water.

contains the third-largest watershed in the world, and it drains into the Gulf of Mexico. A growing dead zone in the Gulf is blamed, in part, on pollution from fertilizer.

Fertilizer pollution can harm humans too. Extra nitrogen in groundwater can get into drinking supplies. Too much nitrogen is dangerous for infants, and it can lead to thyroid problems and cancer in adults. The area with the highest risk of this problem is the Corn Belt.

To help eliminate excess fertilizer, farmers can make sure they apply the right amount at the right time. Also, farmers can avoid spreading fertilizer on the surface of the soil, which is imprecise and wasteful. Instead, they could try techniques such as injection or incorporation, which place fertilizer where it will be most effective. With injection, fertilizer is placed below the soil near the plant's roots. With incorporation, fertilizer that has been spread over an entire field is incorporated below the surface through plowing, allowing it to more easily make its way into plants' roots.

The Clean Water Act was implemented in 1972 to restore and maintain clean water in the United States. Also called the Federal Water Pollution Control Act, this law was amended in 1977 to regulate wastewater from industries and businesses. However, it does not apply to farms, so it has implemented a voluntary program to encourage farmers to use less fertilizer. The volunteer program has had mixed results. Also, in 2013, members of the US Environmental Protection Agency (EPA) started looking at state regulations to see if their water quality standards addressed problems in the Mississippi River and Gulf of Mexico. If the EPA sees holes in state regulations, the agency advises states to revise their regulations on water quality.

As environmental groups apply pressure to reduce nitrogen and phosphorus pollution, so do companies such as General Mills and Kellogg. In 2014, General Mills put out a call for companies to propose ways to increase production while also improving their nitrogen fertilizer use.[5] That same year, Kellogg promised to buy from farmers who optimize their use of fertilizer.[6]

CLIMATE CHANGE

Climate change is causing problems for corn farmers. Not only are temperatures rising, but more extreme weather events are occurring, including heat waves, droughts, and floods. During the Midwest drought of 2012 and 2013, the entire corn industry was affected. The livestock and ethanol industries—the two biggest markets for corn—had to shut down processing plants during that time.

According to the US Global Change Research Program, as climate change worsens, there will be more extreme weather. Corn growth will become more unpredictable, which could affect corn prices. The Midwest economy will be hit hardest because it is where the most corn is grown.

Higher temperatures harm corn by affecting how well plants can absorb water and nutrients. High temperatures also cause corn plants to lose more water through transpiration, which is when water leaves a plant's surface. With increased

Drought-Tolerant Seeds

In 2012, the Midwest experienced a severe drought in which many cornfields wasted away without producing any crops. That same year, DuPont introduced a new drought-resistant type of hybrid seed. It was one it had been working on for 50 years. This seed has a root system that is more efficient than its other seeds, and the plant loses less water through transpiration. In addition, DuPont bred out corn's natural survival instinct, which is to limit how much energy it uses to grow its ears and kernels when it's in the middle of a drought. DuPont's research says its new seeds did better than other varieties by almost 2 percent.[7] In addition to DuPont, Syngenta and Monsanto also produce their own brands of drought-resistant seeds.

transpiration, plants draw more water from the soil, which increases the need for irrigation. Over time, corn yield could go down due to high temperatures. Currently, several seed companies have drought-resistant hybrid seeds available. These seeds may help farmers during dry periods.

Erratic weather can also cause floods. Floods can cause oxygen levels in soil to drop, which can damage corn crops. Plus, the excess water compacts the soil and increases the likelihood of root diseases. With flooding, weeds and pests could grow more, which would affect crops. In turn, this could lead to the use of more pesticides and herbicides. Additionally, if heavy rainfall occurs before crops are planted, soil could erode.

8 | THE ECONOMY AND CORN

Even though the United States is the leading exporter of corn in the world, farmers face many uncertainties: the weather, the market, and the US economy, all of which can affect corn prices. To make sure prices remain stable, the government steps in and assists farmers in the form of subsidies and insurance.

FARM SUBSIDIES

During the Great Depression, many people were out of work and could not afford to buy as much food as they once had. Farmers found themselves with excess crops, which led to falling prices. To make up for the shortfall, farmers tried growing more the next year, but that just made the situation worse. Soon, farming families could not afford to pay their mortgages, and some started burning corn cobs instead of coal in their stoves. Farmers became angry and tried to strike, but there was not enough support from the farming community to organize.

The federal government stepped in to help. In 1933, Congress passed the Agricultural Adjustment Act under which farmers could agree to plant crops on only a certain percentage

Uncontrollable factors can dramatically change the amount of corn grown each year.

Farm subsidies are meant to keep food prices relatively consistent.

of their farms. In return, the government paid them subsidies, or gifts of money. Then the government bought any excess crops and released them slowly into the market. By keeping the supply steady, prices remained steady too. Corn, wheat, cotton, and soybean farms received the most subsidies.

CHANGING SUBSIDY POLICY

From 1933 to 1996, the Farm Subsidy system remained approximately the same. Every five years, Congress passed a farm bill to subsidize farmers and store extra grain. It told farmers how much land they were allowed to plant if they wanted their subsidies. And any excess grain was released into the market at a controlled rate, ensuring that prices remained steady.

In 1994, Congress passed the Federal Crop Insurance Reform Act, which forced farmers to buy insurance in order to receive payments for crop losses. Then in 1996, the mandatory requirement was repealed, but if farmers accepted other benefits, they still had to purchase the crop insurance. If farmers refused to buy crop insurance, they had to forego any chance of receiving other disaster benefits from the government.

In 1996, the Freedom to Farm Act changed the subsidy policy. It allowed farmers to plant whatever crops they wanted in whatever amounts they wanted. The idea was to let the market control prices. But prices fell, so Congress passed a new bill to give subsidies back to farmers. Now subsidies were based on how much farmers grew on average and also on how much land they farmed.

Insurance and Recovery

The 2012 drought was the worst in the United States since 1956. More than 1,000 counties in 26 states were declared natural disaster areas. In Kentucky, corn production fell by 51 percent, and in Missouri, it fell by 42 percent. Nationwide, farmers lost 4 percent of their income because of the drought.[1] However, several things saved them. Many farmers planted both corn and soybeans, so when the July rains came, it saved the soybean plants. Also, because corn prices were high, farmers had planted extra corn. Of the corn they could sell, they were able to receive a good price. And lastly, crop insurance came to their rescue. It paid out $16 billion to farmers for their lost crops.[2]

President Barack Obama signed the 2014 Farm Bill into law after it was stalled in Congress for more than two years.

THE 2014 FARM BILL

The 2014 Farm Bill encourages farmers to plant wheat, soybeans, and especially corn. It ended direct payments—subsidies farmers received no matter how well their crops fared or how much they sold for. In place of direct payments, the farm bill helps farmers pay for crop insurance and allows benefits to be paid for less severe damages. These changes are meant to ensure subsidies go only to farmers who need them.

The bill also includes provisions for the environment. First, it requires farmers to follow practices that are good for the environment if they want to get certain subsidies. Second, it helps protect prairies that have not been farmed by cutting subsidies in half for farmers who use this untouched land. The purpose of this provision is to protect prairies from erosion and other environmental issues.

At a price tag of $20 billion, many people criticize the farm bill.[3] They say farmers should not receive subsidies when corn prices are high. Farmers can earn a lot of money at these times. Many critics argue the farm bill should be dropped. Farmers disagree. They say they need subsidies in case the economy changes and prices start falling again.

CORN TRADE

The United States is the number one corn producer in the world. The amount of exported corn varies from year to year depending on demand from other countries, global economic growth, and the amount of exports from other countries. In the 1970s, for instance, US corn exports

Chinese farmers dry harvested corn in the sunshine. China is the world's second-largest corn producer.

soared to 68 million short tons (62 million metric tons) because of high demand from the Soviet Union and Japan.[4] But in the 1990s, when the Soviet Union broke up and China began exporting more corn, US exports dropped. From 2007 to 2008, as ethanol production rose, the United States had greater domestic demand for its corn, so exports dropped to 20 million short tons (18 million metric tons).[5] Currently, the United States exports approximately 15 percent of its corn.[6]

Because the supply and demand of corn is so high in the United States, it plays a big role in determining corn prices in the rest of the world. If the Corn Belt experiences a drought, as it did from 2012 to 2013, then the United States exports less corn, and the rest of the world experiences higher prices. Some farmers in other countries wait to plant their crops until they find out what US farmers are growing so they can plant crops that will be in demand.

Transporting Corn Overseas

When corn is exported, it travels to ports via river barge, truck, or train. Approximately half of all corn goes through New Orleans, Louisiana, where the Mississippi River meets the Gulf of Mexico, and a quarter goes through the Pacific Northwest. The rest goes through the Texas Gulf Coast, California, and the East Coast. Once the corn arrives at the port, it is unloaded into grain elevators, inspected, graded, and certified. From there, cargo ships are inspected to make sure they are able to safely transport the corn. Then, after the ships pull up to the grain elevators, the corn is inspected once more to make sure it is exactly what the buyer wants. After the corn is loaded onto the ships, export documents are prepared, and the ships can sail away with their cargoes.

9 | THE FUTURE OF CORN

In the future, corn will continue to play a large role in feeding the global population. But its role as an energy source in fuel is less certain. The corn industry will need to address several areas of concern to maintain its strong position in the future.

BIOTECHNOLOGY FOR INCREASED YIELDS

While biotechnology helps create corn seeds that are more uniform, yield greater harvests, and resist pesticides, among other things, it is not without controversy. Some people feel uncomfortable eating foods that have been genetically modified. Even though both the United Nations and the US National Academy of Sciences have determined that GMO foods are safe to eat, many people believe GMOs are still too new for people to understand their full effects. These people contend that while GMOs seem safe now they may turn out to be harmful in the future. Some activists want to ban GMOs in food. Other groups want all GMO foods to be labeled as such. In July 2016, the US Congress passed a bill that made labeling of GMO foods voluntary. As an alternative, the bill allowed companies to include electronic labels. These labels can be read by smartphones, which then display information on any GMO use.

Protesters in Portland, Oregon, demonstrated against genetically modified foods in 2015.

Chemical Resistance

While pesticides and herbicides can help farmers increase production, prolonged use of these chemicals can bring about negative effects. Some weeds have become resistant to herbicides sprayed on corn plants. The corn plants may be safe from the herbicide because they were genetically modified that way, but now, when farmers spray the herbicide, the weeds do not die either. A similar situation has happened with insects. Monsanto created a GMO called Bt corn designed to resist the European corn borer. But over time, the insect developed a resistance to the pesticide contained in Bt. To avoid huge crop losses, some farmers plant non-Bt corn as a refuge for corn borers. By not exposing the borers to the pesticide, the goal is to prevent the pests from becoming resistant to it.

Farmers are planting more and more GMO crops. From 1996 to 2011, these crops increased from 4.2 million acres (1.7 million ha) to 395 million acres (160 million ha).[1] Today, GMO crops continue to expand in all kinds of farming industries, including the corn industry.

The future for corn and biotechnology is all about increasing yield. As the world's population grows, food production will have to grow too. Further research into making corn resistant to herbicides and pesticides will improve yield, and so will genetically modified corn that is even more drought resistant. Researchers at Monsanto are currently working on high-yield corn they hope will grow between 40,000 to 60,000 corn plants per acre (99,000 to 148,000 per ha). This is a huge increase from the 1970s, when corn production was just 17,000 plants per acre (42,000 per ha).[2] To further adapt to the need for corn in the future, crops may be genetically modified to grow in soil normally unfit for plants, including in soil containing high levels of salt. Scientists are also developing corn that can grow underground in caves or old mines.

BIOFUEL UNCERTAINTY

In 2007, members of the US Congress wanted to increase the amount of renewable fuel used in vehicles, so they expanded the Renewable Fuel Standard program. Besides ethanol made from corn, Congress set goals for increasing production of another type of ethanol called cellulosic, which is made from inedible plant material such as agricultural waste, wood, and grass. Both ethanol and cellulosic are called biofuels, because they are renewable fuels made from biological materials. But the cellulosic industry has not been able to meet the goals of the Renewable Fuel Standard. In 2016, less than 1 percent of all the renewable fuel produced in the United States came from cellulosic ethanol. It was supposed to have been 19 percent.[3]

Cave Farming

Researchers at Purdue University wanted to see if they could grow corn in an abandoned limestone mine. It turned out the crops grew well, even with artificial light and higher amounts of carbon dioxide in the air. However, the crops grew so well they hit the ceiling, so researchers introduced cold air to try to keep the plants smaller. It worked. The corn produced just as much as before, but on smaller stalks. This successful experiment proved that corn could be grown in enclosed environments, which suggests that someday corn could be grown in space or even on other planets.

Currently, cellulosic ethanol is too expensive to be competitive with regular ethanol. But it produces smaller amounts of greenhouse gases than regular ethanol. Also, unlike regular ethanol, it is not made from a material that could be a food source. If the technology improves

Cellulosic Ethanol

First developed in France in the 1800s, cellulosic ethanol is made from plant material by converting the cellulose material into sugar and then fermenting it into alcohol, similar to how ethanol is made. With all the manpower and energy it takes to make cellulosic, growing plants to make a sizable amount is expensive. However, two relatively new plants are set to produce more than 20 million gallons (76 million L) of cellulosic a year: a POET plant in Emmetsburg, Iowa, which will create ethanol from corn cobs, stalks, leaves, and other plant residue, and a DuPont plant in Nevada, Iowa.[4]

to make cellulosic ethanol a more viable choice economically, then this makes the future of ethanol from corn less certain.

The Renewable Fuel Standard is set to expire in 2022, at which time the EPA will begin managing the program. This means the EPA could change ethanol targets. Industry experts wonder if the EPA will keep the current goals for corn ethanol, or if it will reduce or even eliminate them. Farmers want to keep producing ethanol at current or greater levels. But gas and oil production in the United States has grown, making renewable fuels such as ethanol a lower priority. The government estimates corn ethanol production will stay mostly level for the next ten years, but that might change if cellulosic ethanol can become a more viable alternative or if the EPA revises the rules in the Renewable Fuel Standard.

A challenge facing farmers is meeting the demands for ethanol corn in years when corn production as a whole is down. The EPA has certain production standards it requires for renewable fuel, and the corn industry works to meet those. If a drought or other disaster occurs, corn

Cellulosic ethanol, center, can be made from a variety of nonedible organic materials.

production might shift toward ethanol rather than food to meet the EPA's quotas. This means there would be less corn for livestock and for food production. In turn, this could raise the prices of meat and corn-based foods. Farmers and the government must strive to strike a balance between the needs of ethanol and the needs of the rest of the corn industry.

SUSTAINABLE FARMING

To ensure future success, farming practices must be sustainable. This means current farming practices must not make it harder for future generations to farm. One way companies are doing this is by encouraging their corn suppliers to analyze how their farming is affecting energy, water, and land use. Plus, companies want farmers to study how they are contributing to greenhouse gas

Coca-Cola

In 2013, Coca-Cola made a commitment to obtain its major agricultural ingredients from farmers who farm sustainably. Sustainable farming methods maintain an ecological balance with the environment. One way Coca-Cola is striving to meet its goal is by encouraging its corn syrup suppliers to analyze how their farming is affecting energy, water, and land use. Plus, Coca-Cola wants farmers to study how they are contributing to greenhouse gas emissions and how much soil is being lost on their farms. Coke's goal is to source all of its key ingredients from sustainable sources by 2020.[5]

emissions and how much soil is being lost on their farms. Companies such as General Mills, Kellogg, and Coca-Cola are encouraging their suppliers to follow sustainable farming practices.

AGING FARMERS

Another challenge facing the corn industry is the number of aging farmers without family members to take over their businesses. While many family farms are staying in the same family generation after generation, others are not. This means that farmers end up renting their farms to others not in the family. And the question becomes, what happens when farmers die without people to inherit their businesses?

Young farmers could buy the farms. But there are not many small- and medium-sized farms left in the United States. Most are large, expensive, and hard to finance. This means young people are finding it difficult to become farmers on their own.

As owners of large family farms age, it can be difficult to find someone to take over.

Keeping farms in the hands of people who know and respect them is important. If farms get taken over by companies or people who do not understand the land or how to farm it, they can cause problems such as erosion, uncontrolled weeds, and water pollution. Organizations such as the National Corn Growers Association help give educational and financial support to farmers.

As the farming industry moves into the future, farmers have many issues to contend with, from which GMO seeds to use to which pesticides to spray to how much water to use in irrigation. But one thing they likely will not need to worry about is a decline in the world's hunger for corn.

CORN PRODUCTION 2015⁶

CANADA
15 million short tons
(14 million metric tons)

UNITED STATES
381 million short tons
(346 million metric tons)

MEXICO
29 million short tons
(26 million metric tons)

BRAZIL
74 million short tons
(67 million metric tons)

ARGENTINA
31 million short tons
(28 million metric tons)

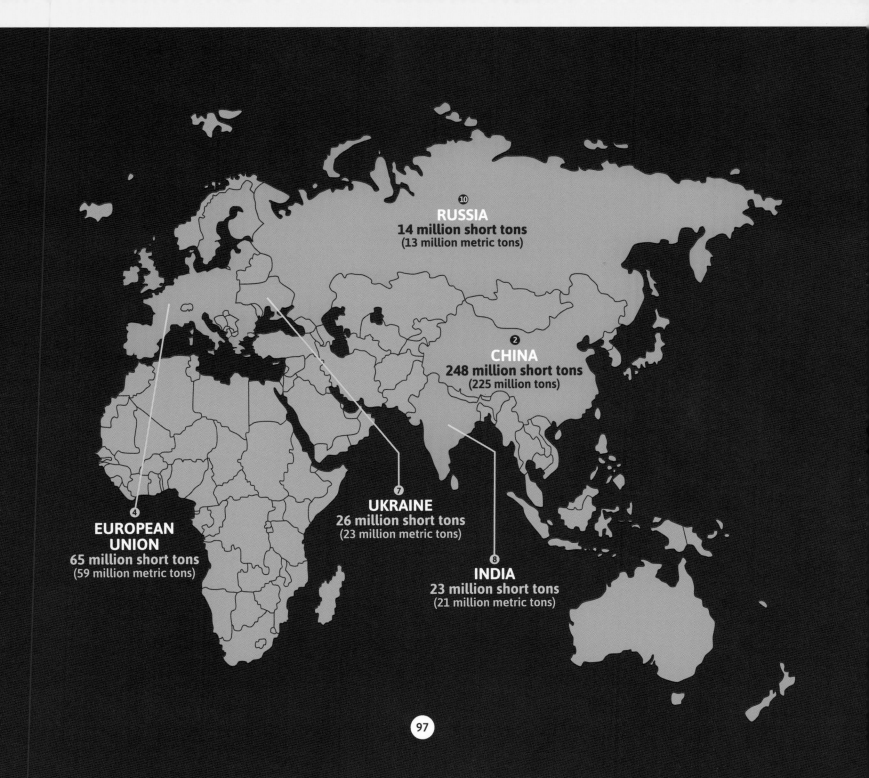

10
RUSSIA
14 million short tons
(13 million metric tons)

2
CHINA
248 million short tons
(225 million tons)

4
EUROPEAN UNION
65 million short tons
(59 million metric tons)

7
UKRAINE
26 million short tons
(23 million metric tons)

8
INDIA
23 million short tons
(21 million metric tons)

Timeline

8000 BCE

Ancient grass called teosinte starts growing in Central America or Mexico as the ancestor of corn.

1492

Christopher Columbus discovers corn from the native Taino people and brings it back to Spain.

1621

Pilgrims learn how to grow corn to aid the Plymouth Colony.

1837

John Deere develops a plow that can cut through tough prairie sod and create neat furrows.

1842

Thomas Kingsford comes up with a way to separate starch from the rest of the kernel by using the process of wet milling corn.

1848

The Chicago Board of Trade is established to inspect and grade corn and to trade corn as a commodity.

1862

President Abraham Lincoln signs the Homestead Act, which gives farmers small plots of land in exchange for a registration fee and a promise to improve the land.

Late 1800s

Corn becomes the dominant crop in the United States. The region where corn and soybeans are the main crop becomes known as the Corn Belt.

1892

John Froelich designs the first gasoline-powered traction machine, or tractor.

1926

Henry Wallace founds the Hi-Bred Corn Company to make hybrid corn.

1930s

Charles Elmer Doolin processes corn into a snack food called Fritos.

1933

The US Congress passes the Agricultural Adjustment Act that pays farmers a subsidy for not planting crops on some of their land.

1952

The pivot irrigation system is invented with a central water source and long-branched sprayers.

1954

Deere & Company creates a corn head attachment for the combine, allowing farmers to pick, husk, and shell corn in one operation.

1970

Monsanto chemist John Franz develops the herbicide glyphosate, which is then marketed with the name Roundup.

1970s

High-fructose corn syrup is introduced into the market.

2005

Congress passes the Renewable Fuel Standard, which sets goals for how much renewable fuel must be added to gasoline each year.

2014

Congress passes the most recent farm bill.

Essential Facts

IMPACT ON HISTORY

As early as 4,000 BCE, corn began spreading throughout North, South, and Central America. People in these areas processed corn into flour, porridge, bread, drinks, and other items. When Christopher Columbus came to the Americas in 1492, he saw the value in corn and brought it back to Spain. In the 1800s, pioneers were moving west into the United States and farming corn because it produced more grain than wheat. From the late 1800s through the 1900s, technological changes made corn easier and less expensive to grow. Corn began being processed into different items that could be used in foods and fuel, such as cornstarch, high-fructose corn syrup, and ethanol. Today, the United States is the largest grower of corn in the world, as well as the largest exporter. In 2015, US farmers grew enough corn to cover the entire country of Germany, more than 90 million acres (36 million ha).

KEY FIGURES

▶ In 1837, John Deere invented a new type of plow that could cut through tough prairie soil and also create neat furrows in it, making it easier for farmers to plant seeds. Approximately ten years later, he formed his own company to make plows, cultivators, and other agricultural equipment. The company grew and expanded its line of products. By 2012, Deere & Company was making $36.2 billion by selling equipment for several industries.

▶ Henry Wallace is known for creating the first company that made hybrid corn seeds. In 1926, he formed the Hi-Bred Corn Company with his brother on just 40 acres of land. Today, the Hi-Bred Corn Company is a subsidiary of DuPont and continues to create hybrid corn seeds.

▶ In 1970, Monsanto chemist John Franz developed a remarkable herbicide called glyphosate. Other herbicides at that time were designed to kill specific weeds. Glyphosate, though, could kill every plant that it touched. Farmers could spray it around their crops, and all the weeds would die. Monsanto called the new herbicide Roundup and began selling it to the public in 1974.

KEY STATISTICS

▶ More than 90 percent of all US farms are family-owned.

▶ The United States is the largest corn grower and largest exporter of corn in the world.

▶ Approximately 40 percent of all corn grown in the world comes from the United States.

▶ In 2015, US corn crops were worth almost $50 billion, which is more than any other crop grown in the United States, including soybeans, wheat, sorghum, barley, and oats.

▶ Most corn is grown to feed cattle, hogs, and poultry. In 2012, this was 38 percent.

▶ In 2014, 40 percent of corn was used to make ethanol.

▶ E10 ethanol is in 96 percent of gasoline currently on the market in the United States.

QUOTE

"I think that farm women are probably some of the most under recognized people out there. A lot of women . . . say, 'I don't farm, I just do the books' which is really a vital part of farming and every little bit counts whether they market or do the books or drive the tractor or bring lunch to the fields."

—*April Hemmes*

Glossary

aquifer

An underground rock formation that contains water or allows water to flow through.

biotechnology

The use of living organisms or other biological systems in the manufacture of drugs or other products.

Btu

British thermal unit, or the amount of heat needed to raise the temperature of one pound of water one degree Fahrenheit.

commodity

Something that has value and is bought and sold.

corn oil

The oil that is separated from the germs of corn kernels.

cornstarch

The starch that is separated out of corn kernels.

distill

To purify a liquid by boiling it, collecting the steam, and letting it cool.

dry milling

A method of processing corn that does not involve soaking the kernels in a solution before they are ground up. Most ethanol is made with this process.

ethanol

A renewable fuel made from plant material, primarily corn or sugarcane.

ferment

A chemical change, often involving yeast or microorganisms, that results in the production of alcohol.

furrow

A long narrow trench made in the ground by a plow.

GMO

Genetically modified organism, such as a corn seed containing genetic material that has been artificially changed to produce a desired trait or characteristic.

renewable fuel

A source of energy capable of being replaced by natural ecological cycles or sound management practices.

repeal

To officially make a law no longer valid.

slurry

A thick mixture of water and insoluble matter.

subsidy

Money paid, usually by a government, to keep the price of a product or service low.

teosinte

A type of wild grass believed to be the ancient ancestor of corn.

till

To cultivate land by plowing, harrowing, or hoeing and prepare for seed.

wet milling

A method of processing corn that involves soaking the kernels in a solution before they are ground up. Most cornstarch, corn oil, and high-fructose corn syrup are made this way.

yield

The amount produced.

Additional Resources

SELECTED BIBLIOGRAPHY

Boutard, Anthony. *Beautiful Corn*. Gabriola Island, Canada: New Society, 2012. Print.

Clampitt, Cynthia. *Midwest Maize: How Corn Shaped the US Heartland*. Chicago: U of Illinois P, 2014. Print.

"Corn." *USDA Economic Research Service*. United States Department of Agriculture, n.d. Web. 4 May 2016.

FURTHER READINGS

Castaldo, Nancy. *The Story of Seeds*. Boston, MA: Houghton, 2016. Print.

Hand, Carol. *Biomass Energy*. Minneapolis: Abdo, 2013. Print.

Hand, Carol. *Sustainable Agriculture*. Minneapolis: Abdo, 2016. Print.

WEBSITES

To learn more about Big Business, visit **booklinks.abdopublishing.com**. These links are routinely monitored and updated to provide the most current information available.

FOR MORE INFORMATION

For more information on this subject, contact or visit the following organizations:

Corn Refiners Association

1701 Pennsylvania Ave NW #950
Washington, DC 2006
202-331-1634
http://corn.org

This organization has operating committees and executives from corn refining companies. It provides education, technical programs, public relations, and government relations for its members.

National Corn Growers Association

632 Cepi Drive
Chesterfield, MO 63005
636-733-9004
http://www.ncga.com

This is a dues-paying organization that works to increase opportunities for corn growers.

Renewable Fuels Association

425 3rd St, SW Suite 1150
Washington, DC 20024
202-289-3835
http://www.ethanolrfa.org

This is a trade association for the ethanol industry. It works to advance development, production, and use of ethanol.

Source Notes

CHAPTER 1. FAMILY FARMS

1. "Meet the Haynie Family." *America's Farmers*. Monsanto Company, 2016. Web. 14 Sept. 2016.

2. "Meet the Hemmes Family." *America's Farmers*. Monsanto Company, 2016. Web. 14 Sept. 2016.

3. Cynthia Clampitt. *Midwest Maize: How Corn Shaped the US Heartland*. Chicago: U of Illinois P, 2014. Print. 187.

4. Ibid. 187.

5. "Corn." *USDA Economic Research Service*. USDA, 3 Dec. 2015. Web. 14 Sept. 2016.

6. Tom Polansek and Karl Plume. "Facing Losses and Grain Glut, US Farmers to Plant More Corn." *Reuters*. Reuters, 29 Mar. 2016. Web. 14 Sept. 2016.

7. "US Select Crop Value." *World of Corn*. National Corn Growers Association, 12 Jan. 2016. Web. 14 Sept. 2016.

8. Rob Wile. "11 Wild Facts about Corn in America." *Business Insider*. Business Insider, 18 July 2012. Web. 14 Sept. 2016.

CHAPTER 2. FORMING THE CORN BELT

1. Cynthia Clampitt. *Midwest Maize: How Corn Shaped the US Heartland*. Chicago: U of Illinois P, 2014. Print. 29.

2. "People and Events, Indian Removal, 1814–1858." *Africans in America*. PBS, 1999. Web. 14 Sept. 2016.

CHAPTER 3. A GROWING INDUSTRY

1. "John Deere Biography." *Bio*. A&E Television Networks, 22 July 2015. Web. 14 Sept. 2016.

2. Ibid.

3. "Deere & Company Annual Report 2012." *John Deere*. Deere & Company, n.d. Web. 14 Sept. 2016.

4. Cynthia Clampitt. *Midwest Maize: How Corn Shaped the US Heartland*. Chicago: U of Illinois P, 2014. Print. 95.

5. Ibid. 126.

6. Ibid. 119.

7. "Biofuels: Ethanol and Biodiesel Explained." *EIA*. US Department of Energy, 17 July 2015. Web. 14 Sept. 2016.

CHAPTER 4. GROWING AND HARVESTING CORN

1. "DuPont Pioneer Advances Next Generation of Corn Products." *Pioneer*. DuPont, 4 Aug. 2015. Web. 14 Sept. 2016.

2. "Statistics FAQs." *The Fertilizer Institute*. The Fertilizer Institute, n.d. Web. 14 Sept. 2016.

3. "History of Glyphosate." *Glyphosate Facts*. Task Force on Glyphosate, 2016. Web. 14 Sept. 2016.

4. "Storing Grain after Harvest." *America's Farmers*. Monsanto Company, 2016. Web. 14 Sept. 2016.

5. "USDA Grading Standards and Moisture Conversion Table for Corn." *Cooperative Extension*. Purdue University, n.d. Web. 14 Sept. 2016.

CHAPTER 5. PROCESSING CORN

1. "Archer Daniels Midland Company Annual Report 2014." *ADM*. Archer Daniels Midland, 27 Mar. 2015. Web. 14 Sept. 2016.

2. "The Corn Refining Process." *Corn Refiners Association*. Corn Refiners Association, n.d. Web. 14 Sept. 2016.

3. Katherine Zeratsky. "What Is High-Fructose Corn Syrup? What Are the Health Concerns?" *Mayo Clinic*. Mayo Foundation, 13 Aug. 2015. Web. 14 Sept. 2016.

4. Brian Scott. "Ask a Farmer: Why Do Farmers Leave Dying Corn in Fields?" *Agriculture Proud*. Agriculture Proud, 9 Jan. 2014. Web. 14 Sept. 2016.

5. Carol Guensburg. "From a Little Blue Box, Tradition in a Jiffy." *American Food Roots*. American Food Roots, 29 Apr. 2014. Web. 14 Sept. 2016.

CHAPTER 6. ETHANOL

1. "Ethanol Basics." *Alternative Fuels Data Center*. US Department of Energy, Jan. 2015. Web. 14 Sept. 2016.

2. Ibid.

3. Ibid.

4. Chris Prentice. "Big Corn Finds Unlikely Allies in US Biofuel Push: Carmakers and Drivers." *Reuters*. Reuters, 23 Mar. 2016. Web. 14 Sept. 2016.

5. "Accelerating Industry Innovation: 2012 Ethanol Industry Outlook." *RFA*. Renewable Fuels Association, 2012. Web. 14 Sept. 2016.

6. "Abengoa Completes $132.4 Million Loan Guarantee Financing for Its First Biomass Ethanol Plant in Hugoton, Kansas." *Abengoa*. Abengoa, 30 Sept. 2011. Web. 14 Sept. 2016.

7. "Pocket Guide to Ethanol 2016." *RFA*. Renewable Fuels Association, 2016. Web. 14 Sept. 2016.

Source Notes Continued

8. Ibid.

9. Ibid.

10. "Clean Cities 2016 Vehicle Buyer's Guide." *Alternative Fuels Data Center*. US Department of Energy, Feb. 2016. Web. 14 Sept. 2016.

11. "Ethanol Basics." *Alternative Fuels Data Center*. US Department of Energy, Jan. 2015. Web. 14 Sept. 2016.

12. "Fueling a High Octane Future: 2016 Ethanol Industry Outlook." *RFA*. Renewable Fuels Association, 2016. Web. 14 Sept. 2016.

13. "Ethanol Basics." *Alternative Fuels Data Center*. US Department of Energy, Jan. 2015. Web. 14 Sept. 2016.

14. Ibid.

15. "US Corn Acreage, Production, Yield, and Price." *USDA Economic Research Service*. USDA, n.d. Web. 14 Sept. 2016.

16. "Ethanol's Effect on Grain Supply and Prices." *Energy.gov*. US Department of Energy, n.d. Web. 14 Sept. 2016.

CHAPTER 7. ENVIRONMENTAL ISSUES

1. Brooke Barton and Sarah Elizabeth Clark. "Water & Climate Risks Facing US Corn Production." *Ceres*. Ceres, June 2014. Web. 14 Sept. 2016.

2. "Statistics FAQs." *The Fertilizer Institute*. The Fertilizer Institute, n.d. Web. 14 Sept. 2016.

3. Tom Philpott. "One Weird Trick to Fix Farms Forever." *Mother Jones*. Mother Jones, 9 Sept. 2013. Web. 14 Sept. 2016.

4. Brooke Barton and Sarah Elizabeth Clark. "Water & Climate Risks Facing US Corn Production." *Ceres*. Ceres, June 2014. Web. 14 Sept. 2016.

5. Suzy Friedman. "General Mills Selects United Suppliers to Increase Fertilizer Efficiency in the Field." *EDF*. Environmental Defense Fund, 21 Nov. 2014. Web. 14 Sept. 2016.

6. "Kellogg Company Announces New Responsible Sourcing Commitments and Renews Conservation Goals." *Kellogg's*. Kellogg Company, 13 Aug. 2014. Web. 14 Sept. 2016.

7. Mike Minford. "Farmers Test Drought-Tolerant Corn Hybrids." *Corn and Soybean Digest*. Penton, 23 Jan. 2015. Web. 14 Sept. 2016.

CHAPTER 8. THE ECONOMY AND CORN

1. Liz Farmer. "How the Corn Belt Survived the 2012 Drought." *Governing*. Governing, 22 Feb. 2013. Web. 14 Sept. 2016.

2. Ibid.

3. W. Robert Goodman. "Should Washington End Agriculture Subsidies?" *Wall Street Journal*. Dow Jones & Company, 12 July 2015. Web. 14 Sept. 2016.

4. "Corn." *USDA Economic Research Service*. USDA, 3 Dec. 2015. Web. 14 Sept. 2016.

5. Ibid.

6. Ibid.

CHAPTER 9. THE FUTURE OF CORN

1. "Biotechnology." *Encyclopædia Britannica*. Encyclopædia Britannica, 2016. Web. 14 Sept. 2016.

2. Ty Higgins. "60,000 Plants per Acre: The Future Corn Crop." *Ohio's Country Journal*. Ohio's Country Journal, 25 Jan. 2016. Web. 14 Sept. 2016.

3. James Osborne. "Political Uncertainty Fuels Questions over Ethanol." *Houston Chronicle*. Hearst Newspapers, 8 Mar. 2016. Web. 14 Sept. 2016.

4. "DuPont to Temporarily Halt Corn Stover Program at Nevada Plant." *Ames Tribune*. GateHouse Media, 9 Apr. 2016. Web. 14 Sept. 2016.

5. Brooke Barton and Sarah Elizabeth Clark. "Water & Climate Risks Facing US Corn Production." *Ceres*. Ceres, June 2014. Web. 14 Sept. 2016.

6. "World Agricultural Production." *USDA Foreign Agricultural Service*. USDA, Sept. 2016. Web. 5 Oct. 2016.

Index

ABOUT THE AUTHOR

Andrea Pelleschi has been writing and editing children's books for more than 12 years, including novels, storybooks, novelty books, graphic novels, and educational nonfiction books. She has a master's of fine arts in creative writing from Emerson College and has taught writing classes for college freshmen. She currently lives in Cincinnati, Ohio.